EXTREME STREET LUGE

TAMRA B. ORR

Marshall Cavendish
Benchmark
New York

Other Marshall Cavendish Offices:
Marshall Cavendish International (Asia) Private Limited, 1 New Industrial Road, Singapore 536196 • Marshall Cavendish International (Thailand) Co Ltd. 253 Asoke, 12th Flr, Sukhumvit 21 Road, Klongtoey Nua, Wattana, Bangkok 10110, Thailand • Marshall Cavendish (Malaysia) Sdn Bhd, Times Subang, Lot 46, Subang Hi-Tech Industrial Park, Batu Tiga, 40000 Shah Alam, Selangor Darul Ehsan, Malaysia

Marshall Cavendish is a trademark of Times Publishing Limited

All websites were available and accurate when this book was sent to press.

LIBRARY OF CONGRESS CATALOGING-IN-PUBLICATION DATA
Orr, Tamra.
Extreme street luge / Tamra B. Orr
p. cm. — (Sports on the edge!)
Includes bibliographical references and index.
Summary: "Explores the sport of extreme street luge"—Provided by publisher.
ISBN 978-1-60870-230-5 (print)   978-1-60870-750-8 (ebook)
1. Street luge racing.—Juvenile literature. 2. Extreme sports—Juvenile literature. I. Title.
GV859.82.O77 2012
796.6'7—dc22
2010017569

EDITOR: Christine Florie   PUBLISHER: Michelle Bisson
ART DIRECTOR: Anahid Hamparian   SERIES DESIGNER: Kristen Branch

EXPERT READER: Rick Wilson, X Games technical advisor, Gravity Games technical advisor, World Cup Championship technical advisor, inventor of Stalker skate truck and first off-road skate wheel xt-wheelz.

Photo research by Marybeth Kavanagh

Cover photo by Chrissie Cowan/Syracuse Newspapers/The Image Works

The photographs in this book are used by permission and through the courtesy of: *Super Stock*: Hemis.fr, 4; *Getty Images*: Shaun Botterill, 7; Mike Powell, 9; Simon Bruty, 18; Philip and Karen Smith, 23; *Alamy*: Buzz Pictures, 14, 19, 20; *KK Photo*: Kent Kochheiser, 16, 26, 29, 40; *AP Photo*: George Nikitin, 25; *Newscom*: John Cordes/Icon SMI, 31; Tony Donaldson/Icon SMI, 34; Steve Griffin, 38-39.

Printed in Malaysia (T)
1 3 5 6 4 2

Contents

ONE

THE NEED FOR SPEED

IMAGINE YOURSELF HURTLING down a street at speeds of 90 miles per hour (144 kilometers per hour) or faster, speeds that would leave most cars behind. You careen around curves. You rocket down hills. Mere inches separate your body from the road. Gravity is sending you soaring, and only friction—and your feet—are your brakes. Sound like fun? If so, then street luge is for you!

← IF SPEED IS YOUR THING, AS WELL AS RACING DOWN HILLS AND TAKING ON MAD CURVES, THEN STREET LUGE MAY JUST BE THE SPORT FOR YOU.

5

Some athletes want to improve their aim with a ball. Some want to learn astounding new tricks. Some want to jump a little higher or reach a little farther. When it comes to street luge, however, there is only one goal: *speed*. Whether lugers are hopping on a sled, practicing high-speed turns, or simply trying to master the skill's needed to enjoy the ride, they all share the same goal: to go *faster*. Street luge is about strategy and skill. It is about racing side by side, elbow to elbow with other riders. It is all about the overwhelming need for speed!

The sport of luging (*luge* is the French word for "sled") has been around for years. The Winter Olympics have included a luge competition since 1964. In this form of luge, sledders race down an icy track with multiple curves at high speeds. The rider with the fastest time wins. Street luge is a branch of this. It is done on a road or street, with men and women competing together. It has been called everything from "road luge" and "classic luge" to "land luge." It is a wild merging of sledding,

STREET LUGE IS AN OFFSHOOT OF ICE LUGE. IN ICE LUGE, SLEDDERS RACE ON A TRACK OF ICE (ABOVE).

skateboarding, and racing. It combines speed and danger to make one of the most extreme sports on the planet.

How it all started is a mystery, with many different people throughout the years trying to claim the credit. Most likely it began when someone sat down on a skateboard instead of standing on it.

7

MEET THE FATHER OF STREET LUGE

ALTHOUGH NO ONE is sure who to thank for coming up with the idea of street luge, all fans know who to credit for making the sport a safer, more respected one: Bob Pereyra (right). In the 1970s, as a teenager, he spent a great deal of time designing and restoring cars. He raced go-karts, and by the time he was an adult, he had been a race car–driving instructor and a motorcycle racer. Eventually he discovered the idea of street luge. He decided to experiment and made a sled that could be used on the road instead of on snow. He traced the outline of his body onto a piece of cardboard and then used that as the pattern to create a light metal sled. He added two sets of skateboard wheels to the bottom, and he was ready to go. He loved it!

Over the years, Pereyra did a great deal for the sport of street luge and for its fans. He designed and built sleds, founded RAIL (Road Racers Association for International Luge), sponsored races, and worked hard to reduce the potential for injury for riders. He even appeared on his board in television

commercials for Diet Mountain Dew, Jack in the Box, and the U.S. Air Force to promote street luge. He referred to it as "skateboarding on steroids" and was known for saying that in street luge, the "motor is in your mind and the brakes are on your feet."

In 1993 the first professional RAIL street luge race was held at the Laguna Seca Raceway in Montgomery, California, now known as the Mazda Raceway Laguna Seca. It was a hit with spectators, and word began to spread about the sport. Pereyra won multiple awards at the X Games. Today he is the founder of SLED (Street Luge Entertainment and Design). The company produces and markets special cameras that can be mounted on luge sleds so the action can be filmed and shared with those not willing to plummet down a slope themselves.

Perhaps she was just playing around; maybe he was tired and needed to rest. No one is sure, but one thing is certain: whoever first came up with the idea of rocketing down a road on a glorified skateboard was a genius.

Race Time

By the late 1970s a number of people were playing around with luge sleds they had put together at home with some wooden boards and skateboard wheels. One of the most popular places to test out speed and skill was down Signal Hill on Glendora Mountain Road in Southern California. During one race a luge sled and its rider went out of control and veered into the crowd, seriously injuring both the rider and spectators. "Bloody Sunday," as it came to be known, served as motivation for safety rules to be put into action—no one wanted to see anything like that happen again. Those new rules included exactly what kind of sleds could be used and what types of safety equipment had to be worn. It also set up racing guidelines, such as where competitions could be held, what precautions had to be taken, and where the crowds had to sit in order to stay out of harm's way.

Once safety issues had been resolved, street luge began to grow in popularity among the extreme sports set. Many people loved skateboarding—but it just was not fast or risky enough. They wanted more! How could they go faster? How could they find a way to pump it up a little higher? The answer was get a lot lower!

ANATOMY OF A SLED – AND SAFETY

HAVE YOU EVER BEEN on a skateboard? If you've felt the freedom and excitement of hitting a decent hill and bombing down it, if you've felt the vibrations caused by every crack in the road, seen the rush of the pavement fly by, heard the sound of the wheels eating up the street, tasted the wind pushing past your face, and watched the world race by you, you have glimpsed a little of what street lugers experience.

When street luging began, riders sat on their skateboards and used their hands to push off down a hill.

That was a fun ride—but it was too slow. Taking a clue from ice lugers, designers began creating boards that allowed riders to lie down on long boards called sleds or simply luges. While skateboards are pushed along by one foot or the other, sleds are propelled down hills and slopes by nothing other than gravity.

PIECE BY PIECE

What does a luge sled look like? First, it is much longer than a skateboard, because it has to hold the rider's entire body instead of just his or her feet. In the beginning, street luge sleds were 8 feet long and about 16 inches wide (although **International Gravity Sports Association** [IGSA] rules allow them to be as much as 10 feet long and 22 inches wide). They had foot pegs on which to rest the feet. The newer **pegless sleds**, also called boomless sleds, are shorter, lighter, and more maneuverable. Like older sleds, they have two or three **skateboard trucks** on them, with up to six **urethane** or rubber wheels. Altogether, the sleds can weigh between 25 and 50 pounds. Early sleds

DESIGNS FOR STREET LUGES VARY, AND MANY ARE CUSTOM BUILT.

were made out of wood, but today most of them are made out of thin aluminum. Some have carbon-fiber aerodynamic fenders in the front and rear.

The frame of the new type of luge is called a **chassis** or a spine and has a **belly pan**. It is built to fit the rider's body. It includes a headrest for supporting the head. It also includes front and rear fenders and bumpers, as well as side handlebars or grips.

There are many different types of urethane wheels from which to choose, depending on the surface and length of road to be ridden. The most common setup is two trucks in the front and one in the rear. This gives the rider the most traction and stability. Although trucks vary, experts typically say the wider, the better.

In the older style of sled, a rider would extend his or her feet and rest them on pegs or a "nerf bar" that is covered in rubber. The new style of sled has a large front fender on it, and the rider's legs balance on the top. This gives the luger more leg mobility when needed and has been shown to be safer in the event of a crash. Handlebars are placed on either side of the chassis or belly pan. They help keep the rider's body in a tight position. They also help the luger steer and keep his or her center of gravity where it needs to be.

Sleds such as these are used by professionals and often run more than $1,000. For the beginning luger, a better choice is a butt board, or classic luge,

THIS RIDER HITS THE PAVEMENT ON A BUTT BOARD, A GOOD CHOICE FOR A BEGINNER.

as it has been called. It is a shorter (4 feet) and wider sled made out of wood. Not only does it cost less money than a regular street luge sled but it is designed to move slightly slower, so a beginner can learn how to use it safely.

PUTTING ON THE LEATHERS

Clearly, riding a luge sled is not like standing on a skateboard. When riders climb onto a sled, their skin, muscles, and bones are not a few feet from the ground but mere inches. Not only do riders feel every bump and rock, they are also in danger of hurting themselves if they get in trouble and fall off the sled.

To keep safe, street luge riders wear "leathers" (one-piece, thick leather suits) that help protect them from scraping skin or breaking bones during a crash. The suits are tight, and they usually come with extra padding in the spine and seat as well as steel plates in vulnerable spots, such as the knees and elbows. In addition, riders wear thick leather gloves on their hands. In street luge the riders use their hands to push off. Keeping them covered is essential so there is less risk of getting fingers shredded or run over by other riders coming off the starting line.

Finally, riders also must wear special helmets to protect their heads. Often these are motorcycle helmets with see-through face shields. The shields keep the lugers' faces and eyes safe from flying debris, or **trail mix**, but still allow them to see the track clearly. One commonly worn helmet is called a "wedge." It has a wide view and an aerodynamic

WHEN STREET LUGING, BE SURE TO WEAR
PROTECTIVE GEAR, SUCH AS A HELMET, FULL
LEATHERS, AND GLOVES.

design, and it is approved by the U.S. Department of Transportation (DOT).

The final piece of equipment riders need are good, flexible sneakers or shoes. Did you notice in the description of the sled that there was no mention of brakes? That is because luge sleds do not have any. The only thing that slows down a luge sled is **friction** and wind resistance. How do riders stop? They stick out their feet and drag them on the ground.

This eats up sneakers, of course! Most do not last more than one race, in fact. Skateboard sneakers work well because of their flat soles, which makes it easy to glue on a layer of extra-thick rubber. In the early days, anything from tires to floor mats were used. Today you can buy precut rubber soles to fit almost any shoe.

A GOOD PAIR OF RUBBER-SOLED SHOES IS A MUST WHEN STREET LUGING. THE ONLY WAY TO STOP IS WITH YOUR FEET!

WHEN ACCIDENTS HAPPEN

WHEN IT COMES TO extreme sports, none is more extreme than luging. It is fast and hard to control. That is probably one of the main reasons there are only about forty professional street lugers in the world.

Accidents happen, and many instructors tell new riders to prepare to crash—not if but when! Their advice to riders is that if they feel as though they are losing control, they should stay with their sleds for as long as possible. Once they finally fall off, they should resist the instinct to curl up and roll. Instead, they are to spread out as flat as possible and use their hands to steer where they go. (And are they grateful for those thick gloves then!)

Proof of the danger of luging was shown to viewers all over the world in early 2010 when twenty-one-year-old ice luger Nodar Kumaritashvili, from the Republic of Georgia, was killed during a training session at the Winter Olympics in Vancouver, Canada. Tragically, he lost control of his sled when he was going more than 90 miles an hour. He flew off and hit one of the columns next to the track, dying almost instantly. In response, Olympic officials shortened the track by almost 200 feet in order to reduce the speed racers could hit. Over the years, many street luge riders have been injured—some quite seriously—and some have died. Luging is exciting—but it is also very dangerous.

FOLLOWING THE RULES

HOW CAN YOU LEARN to street luge? To be honest, you are pretty limited. Street luge is not only dangerous, it is illegal in a number of states. As a luger, you are still like a skateboarder and must abide by many of the same rules. You can't exceed speed limits. You can't endanger others or get in the way of traffic. If skateboarding signs are posted, they apply to lugers, too.

The professionals use the closed mountain roads of downhill racecourses packed with sharp curves for their games, but those are not suitable for amateurs and beginners. Instead, you need to start small, slow, and simple. Sitting on your skateboard and riding down your driveway is a great beginning. (Or you can build your own sled out of simple materials by going online and finding instructions.)

If you want to try a longer track, you might ask your parents to drive you around your city. Take note of parking lots and skate parks. Perhaps a friend, neighbor, or

A GOOD WAY TO BEGIN AND GET A FEEL FOR STREET LUGE IS TO SIT ON A SKATEBOARD AND RIDE DOWN A SLIGHT HILL.

relative has a house with a small hill near it. Each one of these locations is a possible place to work on riding. All you really need is a smooth, downhill surface, but it has to be a safe one! Traffic—whether cars, trucks, bicycles, or pedestrians—can be a real problem, so you will have to research places to go that close at certain hours or tend to be empty a good deal of the time. Of course, having a parent or other adult along with you at all times is essential. Street luging, even in the backyard, is something that requires extra effort to do safely.

It will most likely take you weeks or even months to learn how to use a butt board or homemade sled. You will need to experiment with different push-offs and learn how to steer around corners simply by leaning left or right. It will take even longer to learn how to put out your foot to stop your ride. Since it is unlikely that you will have professional leathers, you should make sure you start out wearing a thick layer of clothes, such as denim jeans, leather jacket, and sweatshirt, as well as sneakers and always a helmet. A mechanic's jumpsuit can work well, especially if you tape the pant legs and arms closed with duct tape.

If you decide that you enjoy street luge, consider finding a local instructor and taking some lessons. He or she will be able to help you find safe places to practice.

STREET LUGE RACERS CATCH AIR AS FANS CHEER
THEM ON BEHIND THE PROTECTION OF GATES
AND BALES OF HAY.

AT THE RACES

When the professionals are allowed to ride and race,
where do they go? Tracks vary from 2 to 12 miles long.
Typically, they are made up of hilly, curvy roads that
have been blocked off from traffic. The sides of the
track are lined with stacks of hay bales to help cushion
any riders who wipe out. Spectators are allowed but are
usually kept behind fences or walls for protection.

The most common type of race is a mass race. Three or four racers ride at once. In super mass races there are six to twenty riders. One of the biggest risks in these races is **tangling**, or getting hooked on one another's sled and crashing. There isn't much they can do if this happens. If both riders are going slowly, they can eventually stop; otherwise they have no control.

Street luge races were part of the X Games from 1995 to 2002. Although they are no longer included, races are still held occasionally in different parts of the United States.

WHEN RACING, RIDERS MUST WATCH EACH OTHER AS MUCH AS THE ROAD IN ORDER TO STAY SAFE.

LIKE MOST SPORTS, street luge has its own jargon and slang terms. Here are a few of the more colorful ones:

AIR BRAKING   holding out your arms, or sitting up to slow down

BACON   rough, dangerous road conditions

DROP A HILL   to run a luge course

FLAME   when wheels catch fire from high speed

FLESH WING   putting out an arm for balance

PUKE A WHEEL   also known as a "melt" or "spew"; to blow up a wheel due to heat

ROAD RASH   burns suffered from scraping the road surface during a crash

SCRAMBLED EGGS   rough but still usable road

SCREAMING MIMIS   the high-speed sound and vibration of worn-out wheels

STOPPIES   stopping a sled in a short amount of time and space

WAD   to crash into a group of people

WAIL   to go extraordinarily fast

WOBBS   speed wobbles or veering too far left or right—usually followed by a wipeout

SPEED DEMONS

WHO ARE SOME of the biggest names in street luge? Not surprisingly, most of them are men— the sport tends to attract more men than women. However, there are a few riders who challenge this assumption. Although Bob Pereyra is considered one of the founders of the sport, other big names include Darren Lott, Biker Sherlock, and Pamela Zoolalian.

Darren Lott holds the Guinness world record for the fastest butt boarding: 65.24 miles per hour. He is a professional racer and the author of the classic manual *Street Luge Survival Guide*. He is a man who does not seem to know the meaning of the words

DARKEN LOTT, A PROFESSIONAL STREET
LUGER, HOLDS THE RECORD FOR THE FASTEST
BUTT BOARDING.

"too dangerous." Along with racing in street luge, he also has been a scuba instructor, a master dive trainer, a shark dive master, a fifth-degree black belt in the martial art Kung Fu San Soo, a rock climber, and a skydiver.

With a name like Biker Sherlock, you can bet this athlete does not stick to spectator sports. Since Sherlock can remember, he has been pushing to see what he can learn to do next. Starting as a child, he rode skateboards, wakeboards, mountain boards, mountain bikes, and anything else he could grab that had wheels. At the age of twenty-nine he tried his first street luge run. The two were a perfect match! "I love anything that has to do with speed, and this is just a really pure, fun rush," he exclaims. He won the first of many gold medals at the 1996 X Games. Over the years Sherlock has started his own skateboard company and even inspired a line of toys called Tech Deck. As he says, "A lot of what I do revolves around speed. In whatever I'm doing, I may not be pulling the biggest maneuver, but I'm doing it as fast as anyone out there."

BIKER SHERLOCK IS A WELL-KNOWN STREET LUGER WHO GOT HIS START RIDING SKATEBOARDS AND ANYTHING ELSE WITH WHEELS.

Going for the Gold

IMAGINE HAVING YOUR face seen by 50 million people every single day! That is what happened to David Dean, the first racer in the history of the International Gravity Sports Association (IGSA) to win the gold medal in both classic luge and street luge. In 2005 Dean submitted a personal story of his accomplishments to a new McDonald's campaign called "25 Stars." More than 13,000 entries were posted online, and Dean's was chosen. Starting in 2007, his picture was on each one of the millions of McDonald's cups and bags given out worldwide. Dean was thrilled and said, "Not only does it give me a chance to work with a brand I love, but I'm hoping it will also help build global awareness for street luging, my personal passion."

THE GIRL IN PINK

If you took a glance at Pamela Zoolalian at work, you probably would not think "risk taker." She is a senior fashion designer for Skatera, an action-sports clothing company for girls. Zoolalian is a small woman, weighing a little more than 100 pounds. However, inside lurks the heart of a daredevil. That love for danger has been there from the very beginning. As a toddler, she jumped on toboggans. As a small child, she was always climbing trees so that she could jump off the roof of her house. As an adult, she jumps out of airplanes, rides a motorcycle, goes scuba diving, and, of course, goes street luging.

The first time Zoolalian ever saw a street luge race was during a telecast of the Extreme Games (now called the X Games). By the time the events were over, she was on her way to buy a wooden board and metal sheets in order to make her own sled. As soon as her street luge sled was finished, she took it for a test run above the hills of Pasadena, California. Her first ride was terrifying—and exhilarating.

LUGING IS NOT JUST A SPORT FOR GUYS. PAMELA ZOOLALIAN HAS BEEN RIDING SINCE THE MID-1990S.

"I was absolutely petrified," she recalls. "You're lying on your back, looking over your belly and across your toes. . . . All I could hear was my heart. I could literally hear the blood circulating through my body." Finally, as she began to relax, Zoolalian said she "started hearing the wind and the wheels. I was hooked!" Later, as she gained more experience, Zoolalian had more fun, but she never lost respect for the danger of the sport. "At 60 miles per hour, you're going 88 feet per second," she explains. "It's kind of a surreal experience, everything flying by you. There's no room for error."

What do all the guys think of this young woman who wears pink leather, pink gloves, pink shoes, and even a pink helmet? After all, this is primarily a male sport. Bob Pereyra says, "She's got a lot of spirit and a lot of heart. She has a lot of friends in the sport. Pamela shows up—it's 50 guys and one girl. She's gotta be tough." The back of Zoolalian's helmet reads "Spanked by a chick." Pereyra chuckles and adds, "Nobody wants to read that!"

GRAVITY TODAY— ROCKETS TOMORROW?

FIVE

STREET LUGERS ARE clearly all about going *fast.* They have a need for speed that seems to surpass that of almost all other sports. Speeds of 70 to 90 miles per hour are often reached by some of the best competitors, simply by them using their body weight and the force of gravity. There are some, however, such as Billy Copeland and Joel King, who felt that going even faster was possible and set out to prove it.

In doing so, they created what is known as "powered street luge."

These men individually worked to find the perfect kind of engine or rocket to put on the end of a street luge sled. This way, when they were racing down a hill, they could fire the rocket and blast off to new speed records.

In 2001 Billy Copeland, known as "The Rocket Man," set a new world record when he lit rockets on the back of his luge and reached an amazing 98.5 miles per hour. That record was broken in 2007 by Joel King when the Nimbus H80 engine, created by the British firm Heward, was added to his street luge. Originally used on unmanned aircraft and to get gliders up to the appropriate altitude, this 90,000-rpm jet engine propelled its rider to a top speed of 114 miles per hour. Joel King stated, "The engine performed beautifully and did everything it needed to do." He added, "The thought of going that speed does scare you, but I was so focused on what I was doing that I had to put the fear to the back of my mind."

BILLY COPELAND, THE "ROCKET MAN," BLASTS DOWN THE ROAD ON HIS ROCKET-POWERED LUGE IN 2001 IN SALT LAKE CITY, UTAH.

Are speeds this fast really necessary? No, but for many riders, they are such a thrill that they could not imagine *not* taking off and letting gravity—

or jet rockets—give them a lightning fast-journey. Street luge is really just for the professional daredevils—and the ones who hope to one day become professionals. Who knows? One day that just might be you!

Taking Luge Further

BELIEVE IT OR NOT, some street lugers are determined to put even more adrenaline into the sport. As if there is not enough danger already, they want to add other risks. For example, some racers prefer to ride only at night. They like the darker hours because there is less traffic on the streets and it is easier to see vehicles coming because of their headlights. Night riders typically put bicycle headlights or "flux lights" on the foot end of their

boards and taillights on the headrest. This allows others to see them as well.

Some riders prefer dirt luge to street luge. With specially adapted wheels, they hit the back hills instead of roads and streets. Typically, these trails are less controlled and involve a great deal more sliding.

For those who enjoy sliding, there is also rain luge (left). Riding in the rain is tricky—and it makes it harder to see and stop. Often it ruins a person's leather outfit—or at least gets the rider covered in mud. However, some riders think a ride in the rain is as good as it gets.

Riders who want to make sure everyone gets to see their rides sometimes participate in video luge. They tape a video camera to their laps and hit RECORD as they push off. Watching their rides not only lets them see what they like to do, it also gives them the chance to learn from their mistakes.

GLOSSARY

adrenaline a substance produced by the human body in response to stress

belly pan plate that goes below the chassis of a street luge

chassis the steel frame of a vehicle that typically attaches to an axle

friction the rubbing of one object or surface against another

International Gravity Sports Association (IGSA) an organization founded in 1996 to foster safe and fair competition for street lugers and downhill skateboarders

pegless sled a luge sled that does not have a foot pegs, or a place to rest your feet

skateboard truck the base that holds the wheels and attaches to the board

tangling running into other lugers or catching on another's sled

trail mix road debris, such as rocks, sand, and pebbles, kicked up by another rider

urethane a type of plastic that comes in different strengths and is often used for wheels

X Games an annual sports competition featuring extreme sports

FIND OUT MORE

BOOKS

Blomquist, Christopher. *Street Luge in the X Games.*
New York: PowerKids Press, 2003.

Murdico, Suzanne. *Street Luge and Dirtboarding.*
New York: Rosen Central, 2003.

Sohn, Emily. *Skateboarding: How It Works.* Mankato,
MN: Capstone Press, 2010.

DVD

Street Luge 101: Beginners Guide to Street Luge, 2005.

WEBSITES

Gravity Sports International's Street Luge

http://gravitysportsinternational.com/streetluge.htm
This web page provides a brief history of the
sport and links to other related sports.

IGSA International Gravity Sports Association

www.igsaworldcup.com
This site provides the most current information
on gravity sports.

Street Luge Sled Construction Directions

www.skateluge.com/streetluge/stguide.html

Learn how to build a street luge at this website.

INDEX

Page numbers in **boldface** are illustrations.

ABOUT THE AUTHOR

TAMRA ORR is the author of more than 250 books for readers of all ages. A graduate of Ball State University, Orr has a degree in secondary education and English and has written thousands of national and state assessment/test questions. (Hers are the ones you liked best!) Currently, she lives in the Pacific Northwest with her dog, cat, husband, and three teenagers. In her fourteen spare minutes each day, she loves to read, write letters, and travel around the state of Oregon, marveling at the breathtaking scenery.